The Mutt
& the Mustang

Based on a true story

By Judy Archibald

Illustrated by Patricia H. Greenberg

To My friend Nick, who is a talented musician & nature photographer,

Judy Archibald,

Kody's Mom

First published in 2011 by:
Pet Pals Publishing
PO Box 1748
Estes Park, Colorado 80517
www.judyspetpals.com

Library of Congress Cataloging-in-Publication Data

Archibald, Judy
        The Mutt & The Mustang written by Judy Archibald;
        Illustrated by Patricia Greenberg
        Summary: small dog, Kody is sad because he fails at tasks big dogs can do. After making friends with
        a mustang who lets him ride on his back every day, Kody discovers by being himself, he is special.

ISBN 978-0-615-45024-7
1. Dogs-true story 2. Horses-true story   3.Pets 4. Animal friendships

                    Printed in South Korea, by Pacom Korea

Dedicated to:

All the horses, dogs and cats in humane societies

and horse rescues who are waiting for their forever homes.

Pet Pals Publishing

Celebrating the Bond Between Animals & Humans

PO Box 1748 • Estes Park, CO 80517

www.judyspetpals.com

Kody, a little mutt with curly gray hair and long floppy
ears, lived with Lilly and her mother in a house high in
the mountains near Rocky Mountain National Park.
Thousands of wild birds and animals lived near the park
boundaries so Lilly told friends, "My neighbors are
coyotes, hawks, owls, deer, bear, and elk."

Lilly helped her mother take care of the little dog Kody, a German shepherd called Cheyenne, two goats, ten chickens, a white cat and two horses named Rio and Raven.

Rio, with patches of white on his reddish brown body and a golden mane and tail, was a paint horse who Lilly enjoyed riding on trails.
Raven, who was black as night with a white blaze on his forehead and three white feet, was a mustang.

Lilly's mother had adopted Rio and Raven from a horse rescue, which is a farm that provides food, shelter and care for horses while looking to place them in new homes.

Cloud, the white cat who was adopted from a cat rescue,
was best friends with the German shepherd Cheyenne who
licked her fur every day.

Every morning Lilly and Cheyenne walked down the
driveway to get the newspaper which the big dog picked
up in her mouth and carried back to the farm house.
"Thank you," said Lilly. "You are a special dog."

When Lilly fed the chickens, Cheyenne carried the pail of grain in her mouth.

"Thank you," said Lilly. "You are a special dog."

When Lilly moved the goats into the barn, Cheyenne
barked at their heels to herd them inside.
"Thank you," said Lilly. "You are a special dog."

As Lilly fed the horses, Cheyenne held Kody's leash in her mouth so the little mutt wouldn't get stepped on.

"Thank you," said Lilly. "Cheyenne, you are a special dog."

While watching Cheyenne help Lilly do chores, Kody's ears fell to the side of his face and his eyes grew round and sad. "Why are you sad?" asked Lilly. "You steal Cheyenne's food and toys, play with the cat and go on walks with me. And I love you very much. Isn't that enough?"

Of course, Kody couldn't tell Lilly that he wanted more. He wanted Lilly to call him a special dog too.

One night, while Kody slept on his bed beside the wood stove, he dreamed about helping Lilly do chores the way Cheyenne did.

The next morning Kody ran down the driveway to pick up
the newspaper but it was too big to fit into his mouth.

Kody then tried to herd the goats into the barn, but the nanny goat shook her head and chased him away. Lilly laughed. "Kody, you are too little to herd goats."

When Kody tried to carry the pail of chicken feed, it spilled all over the ground where magpies quickly gobbled it up. "Bad dog," scolded Lilly.

Kody's head slumped to the ground. He pulled his tail between his legs and ran under the farm porch to hide.

When it was time to feed the dogs, Lilly called, "Kody, come." Too sad to eat, the mutt stayed hidden under the porch.

When it was time to feed the horses, Lilly yelled, "Kody, horses."

Because he loved to visit the horses, Kody scampered out from under the porch to follow Lilly and Cheyenne to the corral.

Rio the paint horse and Cheyenne were special buddies.

Every day, while the German shepherd stood very still,

Rio licked her back and face.

Kody whined. He wanted a horse buddy too.

The next day, while Lilly was brushing the horses, the little mutt stood on his back legs and waved his front paws at Raven. "It looks like Kody is begging to ride," laughed Lilly.

"I guess he doesn't know dogs don't ride horses. Besides, Raven is an old horse with a bad back who bucks everyone off. Even magpies."

A few days later, when Lilly, her mother and both dogs were visiting the corral, Raven was on the ground taking a nap. Kody was so excited to see the horse within reach that he pulled the leash out of Cheyenne's mouth then ran toward Raven.

"Kody, stop," yelled Lilly. "You'll get stepped on."

But the little dog did not stop.

Instead, Kody jumped onto Raven's back then used his teeth to pull knots out of the mustang's mane. "Horses nibble each other's necks as a show of friendship," said Lilly's mother, "Kody's gentle nips must feel good to Raven."

Though surprised to have a dog scratching his back, the horse stayed down.

After the mutt jumped to the ground, Raven stood up then lowered his head to sniff Kody. The mutt licked the mustang's nose.

Lilly clapped her hands together joyfully. "Just like Rio and Cheyenne, Raven and Kody are buddies." she said.

Lilly put a red halter and rope on Raven then lifted Kody onto the horse's back.

"Mama, look," she said. "Raven isn't bucking."

Lilly led the black mustang around the arena with Kody on
his back. The little mutt held his head proudly in the air.
All the while, Lilly's mother, Cheyenne, Rio, Cloud and
even deer at the edge of the woods watched him ride. He
was higher than Lilly. He was higher than Cheyenne. He
was higher than he had ever been.

"Kody is so happy, he looks as if he is smiling," said Lilly.
"I don't know any other dog brave enough to ride a horse."

"Raven is pretty special too," said Lilly's mother. "I don't
know another horse who would let a dog ride on his back."

Lilly lifted Kody down from Raven's back and kissed the mustang's nose. "Thank you," she said. "You are a very special old horse."

Then Lilly picked up the little mutt and gave him a hug. "You are more than a special dog," she said. "You are a mutt who rides a mustang. No dog can be more special than that."

Finally, Lilly had called Kody special. He had a horse buddy like Cheyenne and could do something no big dog could ever do. Beneath his scruffy whiskers, the little mutt really was smiling.

Kody, the author's poodle schnauzer mix (snoodle) rides Raven, a rescued black mustang with a bad back almost every day. After Kody jumped on Raven while he was lying down and the horse didn't mind, Judy realized the two had a special friendship so she plopped Kody on Raven's back and, ever since, he rides every day.

Rio, a paint horse rescued from starvation, has a special friendship with Cheyenne, Judy's German shepherd whom she grooms every day. Cheyenne has a six inch metal plate in one of her hind legs so she can't walk very far. Nonetheless, she never misses the opportunity to walk to the barn, arena or pasture to visit the horses.

Kody, Raven, Cheyenne, Rio and Cloud live with the author in the Colorado Rockies.

Visit **www.judyspetpals.com** to watch a video of Kody riding Raven and Cheyenne walking Kody on a leash.

Horse rescues, which are all over the world, provide care, shelter, food and adoption services for abused, neglected or unwanted horses with the goal of finding them forever homes.

Humane Societies provide care, shelter, food and adoption services for abused, neglected or unwanted dogs, cats, rabbits and other small animals with the goal of finding them forever homes.

A portion of proceeds from book sales will be donated to horse rescues and/or humane societies.

Pets featured in The Mutt & The Mustang

JUDY ARCHIBALD

For more than twenty-five years, Judy has been a feature writer for national magazines, including *Wildlife Art, Art-Talk, Equine Images* and *Southwest Art*. For more than ten years, she has been curator of the annual Colorado Governor's Invitational Art Show. An animal lover/advocate, Judy lives with the dogs, cat and horses featured in this book in Estes Park, Colorado adjacent to Rocky Mountain National Park, where she enjoys having rabbits, elk, deer, coyotes, hawks and owls as neighbors. A portion of book proceeds will be contributed to horse rescues and humane societies.

To watch a video of Kody riding Raven and Cheyenne walking Kody on a leash, visit www.judyspetpals.com.

PATRICIA HENRIKSEN GREENBERG

Patricia grew up in New York and received her Bachelor of Fine Arts degree from SUNY Stony Brook. Her pencil drawings communicate a love of the outdoors and the wildlife encountered there. She relocated to Estes Park, CO in 2004 where she continues to find her creative expression in the natural world. Patricia has illustrated two hand-bound, limited edition books, "Feather" and "Passing Time Along the Gem Lake Trail." She is currently studying Botanical Illustration at the Denver Botanic Gardens.